MATT MORTON
BRIAN FISHER
BLAKE JENNINGS

GIDEON

FROM WEAKLING TO WARRIOR

TH1NK, an
Imprint of
NavPress

Discipleship Inside Out®

NavPress is the publishing ministry of The Navigators, an international Christian organization and leader in personal spiritual development. NavPress is committed to helping people grow spiritually and enjoy lives of meaning and hope through personal and group resources that are biblically rooted, culturally relevant, and highly practical.

For a free catalog go to www.NavPress.com or call 1.800.366.7788 in the United States or 1.800.839.4769 in Canada.

NavPress titles may be purchased in bulk for ministry, educational, business, fund-raising, or sales promotional use. For information please call NavPress Special Markets at 1.800.504.2924.

ISBN-13: 978-1-61291-143-4
ISBN-13: 978-1-61291-422-0 (electronic)

Cover design by Arvid Wallen

Some of the anecdotal illustrations in this book are true to life and are included with the permission of the persons involved. All other illustrations are composites of real situations, and any resemblance to people living or dead is coincidental.

Printed in the United States of America

1 2 3 4 5 6 7 8 / 17 16 15 14 13 12

Contents

Acknowledgments

WE WOULD LIKE to thank the many people who helped us complete this Bible study. Thank you to our wives, who supported and encouraged us during a frenetic year of simultaneous preaching and writing. Thank you to the wonderful elders and staff of Grace Bible Church, who gave us the time to write.

How to Use This Study

ONE YOUNG MAN leads a band of 300 men, valiant but untrained in war, against an army of 135,000 well-armed and experienced soldiers. The fate of an entire nation, an entire race of people, rests on the shoulders of this weak, fearful, and unlikely hero named Gideon.

We hope that studying the life of this unlikely hero will change the way you think about God, yourself, and other people. Gideon's life portrays the phenomenal, world-changing impact of a faithful young man who chooses to trust and rely upon God rather than upon himself.

Studying God's Word has the potential to transform us in amazing ways if we approach it with obedient hearts and open minds. The best environment for any Bible study is a small group of friends with whom you can discuss the questions and passages. We learn best when we have other people to encourage us and to hold us accountable. If you do this study with a group, answer the questions on your own throughout the week and then get together with your friends to discuss what you have learned and to encourage one another to live it out.

Each lesson is divided into four main sections. First, you will find some introductory comments and two or three questions designed to get you thinking about the relevant topic for that week. The second section, called "Look It Over," will ask you to make some basic observations about the week's Bible passage. Third, "Think It Through" will take you a bit deeper into questions about the passage's meaning for the Israelites and its relevance for us. Finally, "Make It Real" will challenge you to apply the passage to your own life. Throughout the lessons you'll find one or two personal download applications. You'll be able to recognize them by the following download icon. Try not to skip these activities because they'll challenge you to really examine yourself and the main points of the week. At the end of each lesson there is a memory verse, chosen so that you can keep the main point of the lesson on your heart and mind throughout the week. If you are short on time one week, ask your leader which portions of the study will be most valuable for the group discussion.

You'll notice that every lesson includes the full text of the main Scripture reading(s) taken from *The Message*, but you'll want to have a Bible or Bible app handy to look up the additional passages referenced throughout the lessons. Be sure to bring your Bible to your group meeting so you can discuss these passages with your friends.

We hope that you enjoy this study and that it is a useful tool as you grow in your understanding and application of God's Word. If you would like more information about Bible study methods or would like to download some additional curriculum, check us out online at www.grace-bible.org.

Matt Morton, Brian Fisher, and Blake Jennings

A Hero for Dark Times

In those days Israel had no king; all the people did whatever seemed right in their own eyes.

JUDGES 21:25 (NLT)

BRUCE WAYNE GRIEVED over the violence and crime that had corrupted his home, his beloved Gotham City. It had claimed countless innocent victims, including members of his own family. As a child Bruce watched in horror while his parents were ruthlessly murdered in front of his very eyes. Many years later, having inherited their vast fortune, Wayne transformed himself into the ultimate vigilante, on a mission to single-handedly stamp out injustice in Gotham. Batman, also known as the Dark Knight, roamed the streets by night and enforced his own brand of justice on thugs and mobsters who dared to prey on helpless victims. With the use of high-tech weaponry and advanced combat tactics, Batman was more than a match for any criminal who would dare to challenge him.

The story of Batman continues to capture hearts and minds, both young and old, because we would all love to be like him: a self-made hero who, by virtue of his strength, wealth, and intellect, fights for truth and justice in the midst of a dark and corrupt world. Batman is the ultimate American hero. He rescues people in need but never needs to be rescued himself. Stories about strong, independent heroes appeal to us because we want to possess that same kind of strength.

This Bible study focuses on the story of Gideon, a man who found the strength to be a hero when his nation desperately needed one. But Gideon's strength came from a very different source than most of our modern-day heroes like Batman. In fact, Gideon's life could not have been more different from Bruce Wayne's. Unlike Batman, Gideon was weak and insignificant. He didn't come from a wealthy background, and he had no special military training. But God gave him the strength for an unbelievable mission: to rescue his people from a powerful and enormous army. He was just an ordinary guy whom God used to do extraordinary things. The time in which he lived was evil, and the problems the nation faced seemed impossible to fix. But as Gideon's life proves, the strongest heroes emerge in the darkest times, and the weakest men are often the ones God uses to accomplish the greatest tasks.

THE PORTRAIT OF A HERO

1. When you hear the word *hero*, what sort of person comes to mind? What character traits and abilities make a person a hero?

2. If you had the power to be a superhero, what would you set out to accomplish for yourself, your family and friends, and the world?

• For myself

- For my family and friends

- For the world

DARK TIMES

The book of Judges begins immediately after God led the nation of Israel into the land He promised them. The people had experienced amazing victories, such as the conquest of Jericho (see Joshua 6). Judges 2:10-23 tells the story of what happened when the first generation who entered the land grew old and died:

> Eventually that entire generation died and was buried. Then another generation grew up that didn't know anything of GOD or the work he had done for Israel.
>
> The People of Israel did evil in GOD's sight: they served Baal-gods; they deserted GOD, the God of their parents who had led them out of Egypt; they took up with other gods, gods of the peoples around them. They actually worshiped them! And oh, how they angered GOD as they worshiped god Baal and goddess Astarte! GOD's anger was hot against Israel: He handed them off to plunderers who stripped them; he sold them cheap to enemies on all sides. They were helpless before their enemies. Every time they walked out the door GOD was with them—but for evil, just as GOD had said, just as he had sworn he would do. They were in a bad way.

But then GOD raised up judges who saved them from their plunderers. But they wouldn't listen to their judges; they prostituted themselves to other gods—worshiped them! They lost no time leaving the road walked by their parents, the road of obedience to GOD's commands. They refused to have anything to do with it.

When GOD was setting up judges for them, he would be right there with the judge: He would save them from their enemies' oppression as long as the judge was alive, for GOD was moved to compassion when he heard their groaning because of those who afflicted and beat them. But when the judge died, the people went right back to their old ways—but even worse than their parents!—running after other gods, serving and worshiping them. Stubborn as mules, they didn't drop a single evil practice.

And GOD's anger blazed against Israel. He said, "Because these people have thrown out my covenant that I commanded their parents and haven't listened to me, I'm not driving out one more person from the nations that Joshua left behind when he died. I'll use them to test Israel and see whether they stay on GOD's road and walk down it as their parents did."

That's why GOD let those nations remain. He didn't drive them out or let Joshua get rid of them.

LOOK IT OVER

3. How did the attitudes and actions of God's people change after the first generation of Israelites died?

4. What were the consequences of their sin and unbelief?

SAME SONG, DIFFERENT VERSE

Some people make the same mistakes again and again without learning from them. We (Blake and Matt) had a friend in college who showed up to class nearly every morning with bloodshot eyes and a half-grown beard. When we asked him why he looked so disheveled, he always responded that he stayed up too late the previous night doing his homework. This puzzled us; we had the same assignments that he did and somehow managed to get to bed at a reasonable time. Further questioning, though, revealed that he wasn't up late simply because of his heavy workload. Instead, he spent most of the evening socializing and playing computer games with his friends and neighbors. He started his homework around midnight and finished his work at three or four in the morning. He then took a short nap before waking up to attend class the next day. He always regretted his decisions in the harsh light of day, but his discomfort never made him change his behavior. He repeated the same pattern night after night.

Similarly, the nation of Israel kept repeating the same terrible pattern generation after generation. Despite the fact that God repeatedly warned them and judged them for their sin, they still chose to pursue their own path instead of His. Knowing a bit about this history will give us a deeper appreciation of God's unconditional love since He repeatedly forgave them and restored them from the consequences of their sin.

»»»

THE CYCLE OF SIN

The book of Judges follows a pattern. The people disobey God, so He judges them by turning them over to their enemies. They cry out in their distress, and God delivers them. Sadly, they quickly forget God and return to their sin and idolatry, which starts the cycle over again.

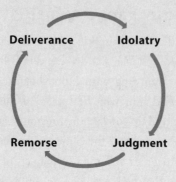

THINK IT THROUGH

In the Ten Commandments, God clearly commanded His people to stay away from idols. In fact, the first two commandments strongly warned the people to worship God alone instead of the gods of the nations around them:

GOD spoke all these words: I am GOD, your God,
    who brought you out of the land of Egypt,
    out of a life of slavery.
No other gods, only me.
No carved gods of any size, shape, or form of anything whatever,
whether of things that fly or walk or swim. Don't bow down to

them and don't serve them because *I* am GOD, your God, and I'm a most jealous God, punishing the children for any sins their parents pass on to them to the third, and yes, even to the fourth generation of those who hate me. But I'm unswervingly loyal to the thousands who love me and keep my commandments. (Exodus 20:1-6)

5. Why does idolatry make God so angry?

6. What does it mean that God is jealous? That word is usually negative when it's used to describe people. So how can it be okay for God to be jealous?

A DIFFERENT KIND OF HERO

As we study the life of Gideon, we'll see that he achieved his greatest victories when he trusted in God rather than in himself. Our culture tells us that a true hero is self-reliant; the Bible tells us that a true hero relies on God, and we'll look at this more closely over the next few weeks. Gideon's life demonstrates that we'll have our greatest impact when we trust in God rather than in our own strength.

The first step to becoming someone who trusts God is to begin a relationship with Him through Jesus Christ. No matter how strong or smart or good we are, our sin prevents us from knowing God and spending eternity with Him; we deserve only punishment and death (see Romans 3:23). Jesus provided the only solution by dying in our place and rising again so that we can have eternal life and minute-by-minute interaction with God. He offers that life freely to anybody who believes in Him (see John 3:16).

The moment you believe in Jesus, the Spirit of God comes to live in your heart and gives you the power and strength to do God's will (see Romans 8:11). When we Christians listen to God's Word and rely on the power of God's Spirit, He shapes us into people who can infuse our dark world with the hope and life that only Jesus can provide. That's what it means to be a true hero.

MAKE IT REAL

7. Do you believe that Jesus died for your sins and rose from the dead? If so, you have eternal life! If not, what's holding you back (an intellectual objection, something from your past, the notion that it just sounds too easy to be true)? Talk to your Bible study leader or a Christian parent, friend, or pastor about your objection.

8. Do you have any strengths or abilities that tempt you to trust in yourself rather than God? Check all that apply or write your own in the space provided.

- ☐ Appearance
- ☐ Athletic ability
- ☐ Intelligence
- ☐ Sense of humor
- ☐ Creative talent
- ☐ Other: _____

9. If you are a Christian, what are one or two specific ways you can exercise greater trust in God on a daily basis?

MEMORIZE

When we fill our minds and hearts with the Word of God, we have protection against temptation. Instead of thinking about sin, we can focus on God's values. In each lesson, we will provide a short passage for you to commit to memory. Don't pass these by; the Bible is most effective in our lives when it is written on our hearts. This week memorize Psalm 20:7:

> **Some trust in chariots and some in horses, but we trust in the name of the LORD our God. (NIV)**

If you are doing this study with a group, recite the memory verses to one another at the start of the discussion for each lesson. Each week, add the new verses to the ones you've already memorized to make sure that you remember them.

The Battle We Face

Yet again the People of Israel went back to doing evil in GOD's sight. GOD put them under the domination of Midian for seven years.

JUDGES 6:1

HAVE YOU EVER felt alone in your desire to do what is right? Often it seems as though everyone around you is engaged in ungodly activities: sex outside of marriage, lying, drug and alcohol abuse, disobedience toward parents, pornography, cheating. Staying faithful to God is incredibly tough when it feels like nobody is struggling alongside you.

Yet we want to be the kind of people whose bravery draws others closer to God instead of pushing them further away. For those of us who know Jesus, the Holy Spirit convicts us of our responsibility to stand up for what is right, for the truth and values of Christ. But that can create a lot of tension in our lives since our world doesn't value what Christ values. The tension of trying to please God in an environment that celebrates disobedience can be overwhelming.

When I (Matt) was a freshman in college, I visited some friends at another university and stayed the night in their dorm room. I was happy to crash at their place until they decided it would be fun to watch a pornographic movie, something I clearly knew was wrong. I remember the internal battle I faced as they were watching the film (and I was lying on my back staring at the ceiling). Should I rebuke them for their behavior? Should I leave the room and go outside? If I left, where would I stay that night?

I'd like to say I was confident enough at that moment to stop the movie and share the gospel with them. It would be nice if I could tell you that they all trusted Jesus and we held a revival in the cramped cubicle they called home. However, none of that happened. Instead, I quietly left the room for a while and struggled for weeks to defeat the lustful thoughts and images that invaded my mind. Although I didn't give in completely to the temptation to lust, I didn't exactly emerge as a shining example of victory.

You and I are not the first ones to struggle with doing what is right in a world of sin. For hundreds of years, the nation of Israel worshiped idols and reveled in their disobedience against God. The period of the judges was the darkest time in their history—the people were out of control. Their persistent sin brought God's punishment in the form of foreign armies that conquered and oppressed them. It was in this terrible time that the story of our hero Gideon took place. Like you and me, Gideon faced a critical choice between blending into the evil culture around him and taking a stand for God's values. Read Judges 6:1-10:

Yet again the People of Israel went back to doing evil in GOD's sight. GOD put them under the domination of Midian for seven years. Midian overpowered Israel. Because of Midian, the People of Israel made for themselves hideouts in the mountains—caves and forts. When Israel planted its crops, Midian and Amalek, the easterners, would invade them, camp in their fields, and destroy their crops all the way down to Gaza. They left nothing for them to live on, neither sheep nor ox nor donkey. Bringing their cattle and tents, they came in and took over, like an invasion of locusts. And their camels—past counting! They marched in and devastated the country. The People of Israel, reduced to grinding poverty by Midian, cried out to GOD for help.

One time when the People of Israel had cried out to GOD because of Midian, GOD sent them a prophet with this message: "GOD, the God of Israel, says,

> I delivered you from Egypt,
>   I freed you from a life of slavery;
> I rescued you from Egypt's brutality
>   and then from every oppressor;
> I pushed them out of your way
>   and gave you their land.

"And I said to you, 'I am GOD, your God. Don't for a minute be afraid of the gods of the Amorites in whose land you are living.' But you didn't listen to me."

THE DESTRUCTIVENESS OF SIN

1. If you were alive during the time of the judges, do you think you would have obeyed God, or would you have conformed to the sinful culture around you? Why?

2. Would you have been angry with your sinful countrymen who brought God's punishment on your nation? Do you think you would have spoken out against their sin, or would you have kept quiet? Why?

3. What are the biggest spiritual challenges you face as you try to
   obey Christ in a sinful world? Circle the ones that are relevant to
   you or add your own in the space provided.

PRIDE

DESIRE FOR POPULARITY

LUST/PORNOGRAPHY

CHEATING

LYING

FEAR

REBELLION AGAINST AUTHORITY

ANGER

JEALOUSY

HATE

HOW IS YOUR CULTURE AFFECTING YOU?

Everybody has a value system. We value things that are important to us, and these values affect our daily choices. For example, if I value looking cool in front of others, I'll spend time and money shopping for clothes. If I want people to think I'm smart, I'll spend time studying. Our values drive our behavior.

Where do these values come from? We choose some of them, but many of them we simply receive without question from our parents, from our friends, from the Word of God, or from the world around us. Often we unknowingly allow the values of our culture to become our own. So many of us are unaware of how we're affected by the images (movies, television shows, and websites) and ideas (books and music) that we regularly consume. The images we look at, particularly for men, have a profound impact on the way we think. If we're not careful, the world will slowly change our values to ones that are at odds with God's standards.

Take a few minutes to evaluate what you watch and hear to determine if you are allowing the values of the world to change you. First, write down your favorite television show, favorite band or musical artist, and most frequently viewed website. Then honestly evaluate your reasons or motivations for each, and list how your choices promote God's values and how they promote the world's values. Finally, determine if you should change your viewing, listening, or surfing habits to be consistent with God's standards. If you want to go even further, do this for your top three in each category.

FAVORITE TELEVISION SHOW:

My motivation for watching:

How God's values are promoted:

How worldly values are promoted:

FAVORITE BAND OR MUSICAL ARTIST:

My motivation for listening:

How God's values are promoted:

How worldly values are promoted:

MOST FREQUENTLY VIEWED WEBSITE:

My motivation for viewing:

How God's values are promoted:

How worldly values are promoted:

Based on this exercise, what changes need to be made in your life (for example, stop watching a particular show, limit your time on the Internet)?

LOOK IT OVER

4. Examine Judges 6:1-10 carefully. What key words and events seem particularly important in order to understand the story? Summarize the main point of the passage in your own words.

   a. Key words:

   b. Key events:

   c. Main idea:

5. What exactly did the Midianites do to the Israelites?

6. Why did God allow the Midianites to harass and attack His chosen people?

7. What made the people of Israel call out to God? Were they sorry for their sin or motivated by something else?

THINK IT THROUGH

8. What did God mean when He told the Israelites, "You didn't listen to me" (verse 10)?

9. Why did God remind the people that He delivered them from slavery in Egypt?

10. How did God expect His people to live in response to all He had done for them?

MAKE IT REAL

11. The Israelites fell into sin partly because they forgot to continually thank God for all He had done for them. Do you live your life as if you are truly thankful to God for everything He has given you? How can you become a more thankful person?

12. Consider your life for a moment. Are there painful circumstances in your life that might be the natural results of your own sin?

Are there sins that you seem to repeat over and over again? What steps can you take to seek victory over these persistent areas of disobedience? Check the ones you intend to do or write your own in the space provided.

- ☐ I will seek honest accountability with another Christian who can encourage me to do what is right.
- ☐ I will remove my access to sources of temptation (for example, get rid of the Internet on my phone, stop going to parties where alcohol is present).
- ☐ I will commit to spending regular time in prayer and in Scripture to train my mind and heart to do what is right.
- ☐ I will talk to my parents, a pastor, or another authority figure in order to help me overcome my sin.
- ☐ Other: _____

If you are doing this study with a group of friends, commit to holding one another accountable to avoid sin and to walk with God. This means honestly confessing your struggles to each other and keeping in contact throughout the week so that you can pray for each other. Remember: Nobody can be successful as a "lone ranger" Christian. We all need encouragement and support from others.

MEMORIZE

For this week, memorize 1 Peter 2:12:

> **Live such good lives among the pagans that, though they accuse you of doing wrong, they may see your good deeds and glorify God on the day he visits us. (NIV)**

Out of the Shadows

The angel of GOD appeared to him and said, "GOD is with you,
O mighty warrior!"

JUDGES 6:12

THE CLASSIC 1984 movie *The Karate Kid* tells the story of a high
school student named Daniel Larusso, who moves from New Jersey to
California. He has a difficult time adjusting to his new school and
quickly runs afoul of the local karate gang (every school has one, right?).
Despite his best efforts to stay out of trouble, Daniel receives more than
one beating at the hands of boys who are stronger and meaner than he is.

One day, however, Daniel discovers that the janitor at his apartment
complex is also a karate master from Okinawa, Japan (again, a common
tale). Mr. Miyagi reluctantly agrees to teach Daniel karate but only if
Daniel promises to completely trust Miyagi's unorthodox training
methods. Daniel agrees, and Mr. Miyagi slowly transforms him from a
scrawny weakling into a fierce karate machine. He is no longer a weak
and fearful young man; instead he becomes a courageous fighter and a
respected leader. Daniel eventually wins the local karate tournament and
the heart of Ali Mills, the girl of his dreams.

Although most of us aren't training to be karate masters, we do
aspire to greatness. But we often feel like Daniel—weak, ineffective,

and afraid. As Christians, we hope to be spiritually great. We want to be the sort of people who boldly proclaim the gospel and bravely stand up for what is right. Too often, however, we give in to the world's pressure to fit in and to simply hide in the shadows. We live like "secret agent" Christians instead of the leaders God is calling us to be.

How can you and I make the transformation from spiritual weakness to spiritual greatness? The story of Gideon provides us with a few clues. Like you and me, Gideon was a fearful person, worried about the consequences of standing up for the truth in a culture that celebrated idolatry and sin. Read Judges 6:11-16 carefully:

> One day the angel of GOD came and sat down under the oak in Ophrah that belonged to Joash the Abiezrite, whose son Gideon was threshing wheat in the winepress, out of sight of the Midianites. The angel of GOD appeared to him and said, "GOD is with you, O mighty warrior!"
>
> Gideon replied, "With *me*, my master? If GOD is with us, why has all this happened to us? Where are all the miracle-wonders our parents and grandparents told us about, telling us, 'Didn't GOD deliver us from Egypt?' The fact is, GOD has nothing to do with us—he has turned us over to Midian."
>
> But GOD faced him directly: "Go in this strength that is yours. Save Israel from Midian. Haven't I just sent you?"
>
> Gideon said to him, "*Me*, my master? How and with what could I ever save Israel? Look at me. My clan's the weakest in Manasseh and I'm the runt of the litter."
>
> GOD said to him, "I'll be with you. Believe me, you'll defeat Midian as one man."

ACCEPTING THE CHALLENGE

1. Have you ever been in a situation in which you felt God was calling you to take a stand for what is right? Describe the situation briefly.

2. Did you feel afraid to obey Him? Why or why not?

3. How did you respond? If you had it to do over again, would you respond differently?

LOOK IT OVER

4. Examine Judges 6:11-16 carefully. What are the key words and events that seem particularly important in order to understand the story? Summarize the main point of the passage in your own words.

   a. Key words:

b. Key events:

c. Main idea:

5. Why do you think the angel called Gideon a "mighty warrior" even though he was hiding in the winepress?

6. What were Gideon's primary objections to God's command that he go and deliver the Israelites?

7. How did God respond to Gideon's arguments?

In some ways, Gideon's story is similar to that of another biblical leader, Moses. When God called Moses to lead the Israelites out of slavery, Moses initially responded with a list of reasons he was unqualified for the task (see Exodus 4). He felt as though he was not a good enough speaker and that Pharaoh and the people would just ignore him. God responded by promising to help Moses in everything he was called to do.

Most of us can relate to Gideon and Moses because we frequently doubt our ability to influence other people for God. We think, *Surely somebody else is smarter, godlier, stronger, or more likeable. God should choose another person.* Gideon felt the same way. God was not impressed, though, with Gideon's excuses. Gideon was focused on his *own* strengths and weaknesses. God was focused on the only important fact: He had commanded Gideon to perform the task, and He would be with Gideon to help him complete it.

THINK IT THROUGH

8. Why do you think God chose Gideon for this task instead of somebody stronger or more powerful (see 2 Corinthians 12:9-10)?

9. Can you think of other times in the Bible when God used a relatively unimportant person to do a very important task? List them here.

10. When God told Gideon to "go in this strength that is yours," whose strength was He talking about? (Hint: Look at verse 16.)

11. How might this reassurance have affected Gideon as he considered the task God had given him?

MAKE IT REAL

When I (Matt) was in high school, my youth pastor gave a talk on the subject of evangelism. He challenged each of us to share the gospel with a friend that week. After his talk I felt strongly convicted to tell one of my friends about Jesus. However, I was terrified of what he might think about me after we talked. Would I lose his friendship? Would he tell his popular friends that I was a freak or a fanatic?

Knowing that I couldn't do this task alone, I began to pray fervently for the courage to share the gospel with my friend. As I prayed, I felt God's strength and peace fill my heart, and I knew that He would be with me when I did His work. Although I was still afraid, I found the courage to talk to my friend. He didn't trust Jesus that day, but he listened respectfully. I didn't become a social pariah. Instead, I learned that when we trust God to do His work, He is faithful to provide what we need.

12. Are there any difficult tasks God is calling you to do right now? Are you afraid? Why or why not?

OUT OF THE SHADOWS 37

13. How might God's promise to help Gideon be an encouragement
    to you?

Look at the list that follows. If God is calling you to one of these
tasks, put a check mark next to it or write down another task in the
space provided. (If you are studying this in a group, apply these principles in
cooperation. For example, start a Bible study together at your school or find fun
activities to do together that you know will please God.)

- ☐ I will share the gospel with a friend or relative who needs to know
  Jesus.
- ☐ I will commit to sexual purity with my mind and body.
- ☐ I will politely decline future invitations to parties where drugs and
  alcohol are being used and consumed.
- ☐ I will start a Bible study with my friends so that we can learn more
  about how to serve God.
- ☐ Other: _____

If you're unsure of where or how God is calling you to serve Him,
spend a few minutes in prayer and ask Him what He'd like you to do.
Then ask for the courage to serve Him as He has called you to do.

MEMORIZE

Commit Proverbs 29:25 to memory this week:

The fear of man lays a snare, but whoever trusts in the Lord is safe. (ESV)

Smashing the Idols

My dear friends, flee from idolatry.

1 CORINTHIANS 10:14 (NIV)

THROUGHOUT HIGH SCHOOL and college, I (Blake) was always an excellent student. God gifted me with a sharp mind and a love for knowledge, and by applying myself to my studies I managed to get straight As in college. That took a lot of work, but I believed it would be well worth it when I graduated. My dream was to find a high-powered, high-paying job in the automotive industry—I had always been a "car guy." And since I knew grades alone wouldn't be enough, I joined many student organizations. I even led an engineering team that built a solar-powered car from scratch! We placed fourth in a cross-country competition with cars from the nation's best universities. To most people who knew me, I looked like an ideal college student who had it all together.

Yet beneath the successful veneer of my life, something darker lurked. My quest for good grades and the best job was really a form of idolatry. In pursuit of the perfect résumé, I made a conscious decision not to be involved with my church or with other believers. I reasoned that I'd have plenty of time for God once college was over. Besides, once I got that great job, I'd have plenty of money to give to the church—surely that would more than make up for the time I sacrificed to school. That's how I excused my idolatry. In truth, I allowed grades and the hope of a great job to become more important to me than my relationship with God. I looked to them to provide the significance and security that only God can provide.

All of us are tempted to worship idols, even if we don't literally bow down before a block of wood or stone. When we allow something (or someone) to become the primary focus of our lives, we are worshipping it. That means that when we are obsessed with popularity, possessions, entertainment, relationships, our physical appearance, or our grades, we are committing idolatry. God wants us to worship Him alone. Idolatry makes Him angry, and it keeps us from serving Him well.

Gideon learned that before he could effectively lead his nation, God wanted him to deal with the idols in his own family. He couldn't be God's man to deliver Israel from the Midianites until he was willing to destroy his own idols. Read Judges 6:25-32:

> That night this happened. GOD said to him, "Take your father's best seven-year-old bull, the prime one. Tear down your father's Baal altar and chop down the Asherah fertility pole beside it. Then build an altar to GOD, your God, on the top of this hill. Take the prime bull and present it as a Whole-Burnt-Offering, using firewood from the Asherah pole that you cut down."
>
> Gideon selected ten men from his servants and did exactly what GOD had told him. But because of his family and the people in the neighborhood, he was afraid to do it openly, so he did it that night.
>
> Early in the morning, the people in town were shocked to find Baal's altar torn down, the Asherah pole beside it chopped down, and the prime bull burning away on the altar that had been built.
>
> They kept asking, "Who did this?"

Questions and more questions, and then the answer: "Gideon son of Joash did it."

The men of the town demanded of Joash: "Bring out your son! He must die! Why, he tore down the Baal altar and chopped down the Asherah tree!"

But Joash stood up to the crowd pressing in on him, "Are you going to fight Baal's battles for him? Are you going to save him? Anyone who takes Baal's side will be dead by morning. If Baal is a god in fact, let him fight his own battles and defend his own altar."

They nicknamed Gideon that day Jerub-Baal because after he had torn down the Baal altar, he had said, "Let Baal fight his own battles."

NAMING YOUR IDOLS

The Israelites worshipped idols named Baal and Asherah. Our idols are often harder to name, but they are just as offensive to God. They might be called Popularity, Good Looks, or Dating Relationships, but they are idols nonetheless.

1. Why do you think God asked Gideon to destroy the family idols before he delivered the nation from the Midianites?

Take a moment to evaluate your own life. What idols are you tempted to worship instead of God? Look at the following list and circle those that apply. You can also write your own in the spaces provided.

Good grades

Dating relationships

Physical appearance

Sports

Popularity

Money/Possessions

Entertainment (video games, movies, televison, music)

Sex/Pornography

Other: _____

Other: _____

LOOK IT OVER

2. Examine Judges 6:25-32 carefully. What are the key words and events that seem particularly important in order to understand the story? Summarize the main point of the passage in your own words.

   a. Key words:

b. Key events:

c. Main idea:

3. How does the idolatry of Gideon's day differ from idolatry today? How is it the same?

»»»

UNDERSTANDING BAAL WORSHIP

The Israelites frequently worshipped Baal, one of the gods of their pagan neighbors, the Canaanites (called the Amorites in Judges 6:10). Baal was a god of weather and fertility. They believed that by worshipping him they would have good crops, financial prosperity, and healthy families. Baal worship involved sexual immorality and violence, practices that God hated. However, the people continued to worship him because they hoped that he would grant them wealth and happiness.[1]

4. Describe the steps that God told Gideon to take when he destroyed the idols. Why is each action significant?

5. What do we learn about Gideon from the way he carried out God's instructions?

6. In your own words, explain how Gideon's father, Joash, defended him from the angry villagers. What did he say that ultimately made them back down?

THINK IT THROUGH

In 2011, CNN published an article about a Hindu temple in Maryland. Hinduism is one of the major polytheistic religions remaining in the world; its people openly worship multiple gods through the use of idols. The article mentioned that in India, a temple is usually dedicated to only one god. But here in the United States, temples often contain many gods because of the diverse preferences of the worshippers. One of the founders of the temple put it this way: "We have a wide variety of congregation and each one of them says, 'I want this god' or 'I want that god.'"[2] His statement highlights one of the key problems with idolatry—we worship gods we prefer rather than the God who really exists.

To many of us today, the concept of bowing down before a statue made from wood, stone, or metal seems ridiculous. There are heart issues behind idolatry, though, that involve more than meets the eye (see Ezekiel 14:3). The worship of Baal and Asherah was no exception.

The people hoped to gain something through idol worship that wasn't so different from the things we chase after today.

7. What was the heart issue behind the idolatry of the Israelites? [Hint: What did they hope Baal would give to them in exchange for worshipping him? Why was this important to them?]

8. In Judges 2:17 God compares idol worship to adultery and prostitution. Why does He make that comparison? How are the two sins similar (see Hosea 2:4-5,8)?

9. Why do you think the people of Israel kept returning to their idols over and over again, even though God kept punishing them for it? In other words, why wasn't God's judgment enough incentive for them to stop what they were doing?

MAKE IT REAL

Despite all of my (Blake's) effort and success in college, I didn't find the high-powered, high-paying job I had hoped for when I graduated. A financial recession that started in Asia six months before my graduation led to a worldwide slowdown in the automotive industry. As a result, I had to settle for a job that lacked both pay and excitement. I ended up drawing shafts and brackets for nine or more hours a day! Disillusionment quickly set in. I learned the hard way that, like all idols, the gods of good grades and career ambition will let you down. Nobody and nothing other than God is capable of meeting our need for purpose, security, and significance. I began to reexamine my life, confess my idolatry, and recommit myself to worshipping and serving God alone.

Gideon experienced a similar transformation. Before God could use Gideon to lead the nation, he had to deal with the idols in his own home. In the same way, God is calling you and me to remove the idols from our hearts before we begin to lead others.

10. Return to your list of personal idols from the beginning of the chapter. What do you hope to gain when you worship each of these idols?

11. What steps do you need to take in order to remove the idols from your heart and make God the center of your life (for example, spend less money on your appearance and give some away to your church, spend less time on video games and entertainment to have more time for serving others, ask God to help you with your anxiety about what others think about you)?

12. Spend some time alone praying that God will help you make Him the main priority in your life.

If you are doing this study with a group, hold one another accountable in the next few weeks as you seek to change your priorities. For example, if you're tempted to worship your grades, the others in your group can challenge you to seek balance in the ways you spend your time. They can ask you on a weekly basis if you have been praying about your anxiety and fear about school. This kind of accountability requires honesty and humility, but it's well worth it to have friends who can help us grow closer to the Lord.

MEMORIZE
For this week, memorize Colossians 3:5:

Put to death, therefore, whatever belongs to your earthly nature: sexual immorality, impurity, lust, evil desires and greed, which is idolatry. (NIV)

Confidence in God's Calling

Then I heard the voice of the Master: "Whom shall I send?
Who will go for us?" I spoke up, "I'll go. Send me!"

ISAIAH 6:8

CHARLES (C. T.) STUDD was a man's man; he even had a manly name! In 1883, Studd captained the Cambridge cricket team at a time when cricket was the most popular game in Britain. He rose to become one of the greatest sportsmen in the country. Young men everywhere knew his name and idolized him.

Yet deep in Studd's heart, he knew he wasn't right with God. Although he became a Christian as a young man, his walk with God remained shallow and superficial. He attended church and occasional prayer meetings, but in reality he loved the world and the fame that came through playing cricket.

In November of 1883, he had an experience that dramatically changed his life. His brother George (also a popular cricket player) became gravely ill and nearly died. Charles realized that accolades and fame and athletic ability were useless to George in the face of death. Both brothers needed a reorientation of their values; they needed to find something they could invest their time and energy into that would last beyond this short life. His brother miraculously recovered, but Charles was never the same. He decided from that point on to invest his life in obeying Jesus and spreading the gospel around the world.

By 1885, Studd and six of his friends (now known as the Cambridge Seven) made the decision to spend their lives sharing the gospel in China. They traded their comfortable and prestigious lives in England for lives of obscurity and struggle in a foreign land. God used them to spark revival through Great Britain and to motivate hundreds of young men and women to become missionaries around the world.[1]

What could motivate seven gifted, intelligent young men to make the seemingly absurd choice to trade their homes and promising careers for the life of a foreign missionary? They each possessed an inescapable conviction that God had called them to participate in the Great Commission of Matthew 28:19-20: "Therefore go and make disciples of all nations, baptizing them in the name of the Father and of the Son and of the Holy Spirit, and teaching them to obey everything I have commanded you. And surely I am with you always, to the very end of the age" (NIV). Jesus had promised to be with them as they fulfilled His command, so they had nothing to fear as they boldly stepped out in faith. Since they believed that God wanted them to share the gospel around the world, they were confident He would empower them for the task.

Like Studd and his friends, Gideon faced his own moment of decision. God's Spirit prompted Gideon to call together the Israelites to fight (see Judges 6:33-35), but would he trust His promise to deliver the Israelites from Midian, even though the enemy was stronger and more numerous? After all, Gideon was just one man, and an unimportant one at that. Would he respond in faith and boldness to God's clear call to lead, or would he shrink back in fear? As you read Judges 6:36-40 consider whether Gideon's response to God illustrates trust, doubt, or a bit of both:

Gideon said to God, "If this is right, if you are using me to save Israel as you've said, then look: I'm placing a fleece of wool on the threshing floor. If dew is on the fleece only, but the floor is dry, then I know that you will use me to save Israel, as you said."

That's what happened. When he got up early the next morning, he wrung out the fleece—enough dew to fill a bowl with water!

Then Gideon said to God, "Don't be impatient with me, but let me say one more thing. I want to try another time with the fleece. But this time let the fleece stay dry, while the dew drenches the ground."

God made it happen that very night. Only the fleece was dry while the ground was wet with dew.

GRAPPLING WITH GOD'S COMMANDS AND PROMISES

1. According to the passages that follow, what are some things God has clearly called us to do, and what promises accompany His commands?

   a. Matthew 28:18-20
      God's command(s):

      God's promise(s):

   b. 1 Corinthians 10:6-14
      God's command(s):

God's promise(s):

c. 2 Timothy 4:5-8
  God's command(s):

God's promise(s):

2. Can you think of any other clear commands and promises of God that apply to you and me today?

3. Why do you think we don't always do what God has clearly called us to do? Why is it so difficult to obey His commands and trust His promises?

LOOK IT OVER

Sometimes Christians ask God for signs, even though we know what He's called us to do. For example, some young men promise to stop looking at pornography *if* God will remove their feelings of temptation altogether. But the Scripture is clear that God wants us to be pure in our minds and hearts even though we will always struggle with temptation (see Matthew 5:27-28). God tells us to flee from temptation and promises a way of escape (see 1 Corinthians 10:13), but He never promises to remove temptation altogether. Sometimes when we test God by asking for signs, we simply reveal either our unwillingess to obey His commands or our lack of faith in His promises.

When God commanded Gideon to lead the Israelites into battle, Gideon didn't directly defy God or refuse to obey Him. But his request for multiple signs indicated that he wasn't fully convinced of God's ability to provide the promised victory. Like us, Gideon had to learn to have complete confidence in God's promises.

4. Examine Judges 6:36-40 carefully. What are the key words and events that seem particularly important in order to understand the story? Summarize the main point of the passage in your own words.

a. Key words:

b. Key events:

c. Main idea:

5. Gideon had just finished smashing his family's idols, a bold display of trust. Why do you think he was still wrestling with fear about the upcoming battle?

6. Spend a few minutes comparing the responses of other men and women of the Bible when God asked them to perform difficult tasks. For each passage, answer the following questions:

- What was God calling him or her to do?
- How did the person respond?
- Why did he or she respond that way?
- How did God respond to each person? Why?

a. Zechariah (see Luke 1:11-20)

b. Mary (see Luke 1:26-38)

c. Isaiah (see Isaiah 6:1-10)

d. Moses (see Exodus 3:1-14; 4:1-17)

THINK IT THROUGH

7. What do we learn about God's character from His responses to the people you just read about? In other words, what do His actions and words tell us about Him?

8. Look up the passages that follow. Next to each reference, write down what that passage tells us about the consequences of refusing to obey God's commands.

- 2 Thessalonians 3:13-15

- Romans 6:16

- 1 Corinthians 3:10-15

- 1 John 1:6-10

MAKE IT REAL

Gideon struggled with obeying God because he was deeply insecure. He doubted his own ability to be the military leader God was calling him to be. He doubted whether anybody would even listen to him since he was the youngest member of an insignificant family. Instead of relying on God's strength, Gideon kept looking at his own weaknesses and allowing them to cloud his judgment.

Nearly everyone can relate to Gideon's struggle. No matter how fearless and brave we may act, we all struggle with fear and insecurity at times. When God challenges us to share the gospel, make a sacrifice, or take a stand for what is right, we are often tempted to focus on our own weaknesses instead of God's strength. As a result, we become paralyzed and afraid to obey. However, when we take the focus off of ourselves and remember God's power and promises, we can find the courage to obey Him. Fortunately for us, and for Gideon, God is extremely patient as we learn how to trust.

9. Have you ever felt inadequate for something you knew you were called to do? Explain.

10. Which of God's commands do you feel afraid of or unwilling to obey? Why?

11. How can you overcome your fears and boldly obey the Lord? What do you need to think, believe, or do differently?

In the space that follows, make a plan to deliberately obey God's clear call for your life.

☐ What God is calling me to do:

☐ Why I am afraid to do it:

☐ Steps I need to take to overcome my fears and obey (get training, seek advice, learn the Scriptures better, just do it):

MEMORIZE

For this week, memorize Isaiah 6:8 with your group:

And then I heard the voice of the Master: "Whom shall I send? Who will go for us?" I spoke up, "I'll go. Send me!"

Relying on God's Strength

"Not by might nor by power, but by my Spirit," says the LORD Almighty.

ZECHARIAH 4:6 (NIV)

IN THE EARLY-MORNING hours of March 6, 1836, 2,400 well-armed soldiers of the Mexican army prepared their assault on a small Spanish mission defended by fewer than 200 Texans.[1] Yet what the defenders lacked in numbers, they compensated for in bravery. They were ready to die, if necessary, to protect their land and the people they loved.

Their commander, William B. Travis, stood in front of them and spoke the cruel truth: "We must die. Our business is not to make a fruitless effort to save our lives, but to choose the manner of our death."[2] According to legend, he drew a line in the sand and asked his men to cross the line if they were willing to stay and fight. Any who were afraid could leave before the battle began. All but one stayed.[3]

Despite the enormous odds against them, the defenders repulsed the first two assaults and inflicted enormous casualties on the opposing army. But the third assault proved too much. The Mexican army breached the walls of the Alamo and killed nearly everyone inside.[4]

Although the bravery of the Texans who died at the Alamo is still celebrated today, the battle also illustrates a harsh reality of war: The army with vastly greater numbers and superior weaponry will almost always win.

Perhaps Gideon had that reality in mind as he prepared to face the Midianite warriors. The Israelite army numbered only 32,000 soldiers; the Midianites numbered 135,000. The Israelites were on foot; the Midianites rode on camels, the tanks of that age. It was a situation bound to strike fear into the heart of the bravest warrior. Yet, surprisingly, God had a plan that would make the situation appear even more hopeless to Gideon. Read about God's instructions to Gideon on the morning of the battle (Judges 7:1-8):

Jerub-Baal (Gideon) got up early the next morning, all his troops right there with him. They set up camp at Harod's Spring. The camp of Midian was in the plain, north of them near the Hill of Moreh.

GOD said to Gideon, "You have too large an army with you. I can't turn Midian over to them like this—they'll take all the credit, saying, 'I did it all myself,' and forget about me. Make a public announcement: 'Anyone afraid, anyone who has any qualms at all, may leave Mount Gilead now and go home.'" Twenty-two companies headed for home. Ten companies were left.

GOD said to Gideon: "There are still too many. Take them down to the stream and I'll make a final cut. When I say, 'This one goes with you,' he'll go. When I say, 'This one doesn't go,' he won't go." So Gideon took the troops down to the stream.

GOD said to Gideon: "Everyone who laps with his tongue, the way a dog laps, set on one side. And everyone who kneels to drink, drinking with his face to the water, set to the other side." Three hundred lapped with their tongues from their cupped hands. All the rest knelt to drink.

God said to Gideon: "I'll use the three hundred men who lapped at the stream to save you and give Midian into your hands. All the rest may go home."

After Gideon took all their provisions and trumpets, he sent all the Israelites home. He took up his position with the three hundred. The camp of Midian stretched out below him in the valley.

A MATTER OF TRUST

God's instructions must have sounded absurd to Gideon. The Israelites were already heavily outnumbered, yet God told him to send 98 percent of his army home, leaving a meager 300 men. That gave the Midianites a 450 to 1 numerical advantage, almost 40 times better than the overwhelming advantage of the Mexican army at the Alamo! Yet God was clear that victory would come by His power and not by the military strength of His people.

1. Can you think of times when you had to do something that seemed impossibly difficult? How did you respond?

2. What strengths and abilities (athletic talent, intelligence, a winning personality) do you tend to rely on in difficult times?

LOOK IT OVER (PART 1)

3. Examine Judges 7:1-8 carefully. What are the key words and events that seem particularly important in order to understand the story? Summarize the main point of the passage in your own words.

a. Key words:

b. Key events:

c. Main idea:

4. Explain in your own words what God instructed Gideon to do in this passage. Why did God care so much about the number of soldiers in Gideon's army?

5. What does this passage tell you about the character and capabilities of God?

A GOD WHO CALMS FEARS

At this point in the story, God had already promised Gideon certain victory over the Midianites. Yet that promise did not remove all of Gideon's fear. After all, who wouldn't be scared of going to war against such an astronomically superior army? Before he could feel confident, Gideon needed further reassurance that God's promise could be trusted. God could have simply told Gideon to "man up" and stop worrying. Instead, He chose to graciously provide him with one final supernatural sign to calm Gideon's fears:

> That night, GOD told Gideon: "Get up and go down to the camp. I've given it to you. If you have any doubts about going down, go down with Purah your armor bearer; when you hear what they're saying, you'll be bold and confident." He and his armor bearer Purah went down near the place where sentries were posted. Midian and Amalek, all the easterners, were spread out on the plain like a swarm of locusts. And their camels! Past counting, like grains of sand on the seashore!
>
> Gideon arrived just in time to hear a man tell his friend a dream. He said, "I had this dream: A loaf of barley bread tumbled into the Midianite camp. It came to the tent and hit it so hard it collapsed. The tent fell!"
>
> His friend said, "This has to be the sword of Gideon son of Joash, the Israelite! God has turned Midian—the whole camp!—over to him."

When Gideon heard the telling of the dream and its interpretation, he went to his knees before God in prayer. Then he went back to the Israelite camp and said, "Get up and get going! GOD has just given us the Midianite army!" (Judges 7:9-15)

LOOK IT OVER (PART 2)

6. Examine Judges 7:9-15 carefully. What are the key words and events that seem particularly important in order to understand the story? Summarize the main point of the passage in your own words.

   a. Key words:

   b. Key events:

   c. Main idea:

7. Why do you think the author of Judges told again how enormous the Midianite army was with their camels and reinforcements from Amalek?

8. Describe in your own words what God did for Gideon in this passage.

9. How did Gideon respond to the dream and its interpretation? Why did he respond that way?

10. What does this passage tell you about God's character and capabilities?

THINK IT THROUGH

11. When you look at the two sections of Scripture you've just read, what is the big idea that ties them both together? In other words, how are they connected?

12. In the first passage, why did God care whether or not His people credited themselves with the victory? Why did He demand the credit? Is God prideful? Is He insecure? Or is there something else motivating these instructions?

13. Why do you think the dream and its interpretation finally completely calmed Gideon's fears, when the previous signs God gave him did not?

MAKE IT REAL

Throughout high school and college, I (Matt) often trusted in my natural abilities as a musician and public speaker to give me success and significance. In the moments of fear that always accompany a public performance, I was tempted to rely on my talents rather than on God to bless my efforts. When people responded to God while I was singing or speaking, I often convinced myself that they were really responding to *me.* I attributed God's work to my own strengths, which was the exact attitude that God wanted the Israelites to avoid.

We all struggle with pride, believing that our own efforts and strengths will provide us with success and significance. But God wants us to trust in Him alone even in the hardest times of life and to realize that nothing of spiritual significance can happen apart from His power (see John 15:5).

14. Fill in the blank: I am tempted to trust in _____ instead of in God to provide me with a life of success.

 Spend some time in prayer doing the following:

a. Acknowledge to God that all of your strengths are simply gifts
   from Him.
b. Ask God to help you trust in Him to provide your life with significance.
c. Commit to God that you will privately and publicly give Him the credit
   for everything He accomplishes through you or the abilities He's
   given you.

MEMORIZE

For this week, memorize 1 Corinthians 4:7:

For who makes you different from anyone else? What do you have that you did not receive? And if you did receive it, why do you boast as though you did not? (NIV)

How Underdogs Become Victorious

He said to me, "My grace is sufficient for you, for my power is made perfect in weakness." Therefore I will boast all the more gladly about my weaknesses, so that Christ's power may rest on me.

2 CORINTHIANS 12:9 (NIV)

ONE OF THE most dramatic underdog stories in Olympic history occurred during the 1980 Winter Games in Lake Placid, New York. The Soviet ice hockey team, heavily favored for the gold, had won every Winter Olympics since 1964. Though technically composed of amateurs in accordance with Olympic rules, some members of the Soviet team practiced and played hockey full-time through the financial support of their government. In stark contrast, the Americans fielded a team of relatively inexperienced college players, only one of whom had ever played hockey at the Olympic level. At an exhibition match two weeks before the Olympics, the Soviet squad crushed the Americans 10–3. After that, most people didn't even expect the United States to advance to the medal round.[1]

But they were wrong. The American coach, Herb Brooks, compensated for his players' inexperience with a grueling regimen of practice and physical workouts. He brought out their best by pushing them to work harder than any other team on the ice. To everybody's surprise, his strategy paid off, and the American team successfully fought its way to the gold medal game against the Soviets, a game so stunning that it became known simply as the "miracle on ice." After keeping the game close for two periods, the Americans scored the go-ahead goal over the bewildered Soviets. As the final seconds of the game ran out, the crowd and the country went wild. The hard-working American team had achieved one of the greatest upsets of all time against their greatest rivals.

We all love when an underdog wins, because we're reminded that physical strength and talent do not always win out. Gideon's victory over the Midianites stands as one of the greatest underdog stories of all time: 300 unarmed Israelite soldiers conquering the 135,000-strong Midianite army! But unlike the American hockey team, the Israelites did not win through hard work or tenacity. Instead, God gave them the victory as an amazing display of His power. Read Judges 7:16-25:

> He divided the three hundred men into three companies. He gave each man a trumpet and an empty jar, with a torch in the jar. He said, "Watch me and do what I do. When I get to the edge of the camp, do exactly what I do. When I and those with me blow the trumpets, you also, all around the camp, blow your trumpets and shout, 'For GOD and for Gideon!'"
>
> Gideon and his hundred men got to the edge of the camp at the beginning of the middle watch, just after the sentries had been posted. They blew the trumpets, at the same time smashing the jars they carried. All three companies blew the trumpets and broke the jars. They held the torches in their left hands and the trumpets in their right hands, ready to blow, and shouted, "A sword for GOD and for Gideon!" They were stationed all around the camp, each man at his post. The whole Midianite camp jumped to its feet. They yelled and fled. When the three hundred blew the trumpets, GOD aimed each Midianite's sword

against his companion, all over the camp. They ran for their lives—to Beth Shittah, toward Zererah, to the border of Abel Meholah near Tabbath.

Israelites rallied from Naphtali, from Asher, and from all over Manasseh. They had Midian on the run.

Gideon then sent messengers through all the hill country of Ephraim, urging them, "Come down against Midian! Capture the fords of the Jordan at Beth Barah."

So all the men of Ephraim rallied and captured the fords of the Jordan at Beth Barah. They also captured the two Midianite commanders Oreb (Raven) and Zeeb (Wolf). They killed Oreb at Raven Rock; Zeeb they killed at Wolf Winepress. And they pressed the pursuit of Midian. They brought the heads of Oreb and Zeeb to Gideon across the Jordan.

VICTORY THROUGH GOD'S POWER

1. If you were one of Gideon's soldiers, how would you have felt about his battle plan? What risks did his plan entail?

2. a. God has promised us victory in many areas of life. In the following checklist, mark the areas in which you struggle to trust God. In other words, do you feel as though any of these victories are beyond hope for you?

   ☐ Trusting God for victory over a particular sin, whether lust, pride, greed, anxiety, or another (see 1 Corinthians 10:13)

☐ Trusting God to give me boldness and wisdom to share the gospel with my friends and family (see John 15:26-27; Matthew 28:18-20)

☐ Trusting God to meet all of my needs and help me overcome my anxiety about them (see Matthew 6:31-34; Philippians 4:19)

☐ Other: _____

b. Why do you think you struggle to believe God's promises of success in these areas of life?

LOOK IT OVER

3. Examine Judges 7:16-25 carefully. What are the key words and events that seem particularly important in order to understand the story? Summarize the main point of the passage in your own words.

a. Key words:

b. Key events:

c. Main idea:

4. Describe in your own words the battle plan used by Gideon and his men. Note the details, including location and timing.

5. Do you see any clues in the passage that indicate that God, rather than Gideon, was really responsible for the Israelite victory? How might the battle have gone differently if God was not involved?

THINK IT THROUGH

6. Was there any logic to this battle plan? In other words, why might this have been a good plan for Gideon's army to use?

7. Why do you think God provoked the Midianites to kill one another, instead of allowing the Israelites to kill them all?

8. Can you think of any other times throughout Scripture in which God used a very strange battle plan to help His people defeat a formidable enemy? Why do you think God often works this way?

9. We believe in a gracious and forgiving God. So why did God bring about the death of so many Midianites (at least 120,000 killed according to Judges 8:10)? Why would God not only condone but actually empower such a slaughter?

MAKE IT REAL

As followers of Christ, we often feel like underdogs living in a hostile world. Our commitment to Jesus comes under ridicule and attack when we turn on the television, surf the Internet, or simply talk to our friends at school. Sometimes it seems impossible to live righteously and faithfully in this kind of an environment. But victory over sin is always possible if we rely, as Gideon did, on God's power. For those who have trusted in Jesus, this power is found through the Holy Spirit, who lives within us. Romans 8:11 says, "And if the Spirit of him who raised Jesus from the dead is living in you, he who raised Christ from the dead will also give life to your mortal bodies through his Spirit, who lives in you" (NIV). In other words, God's Spirit lives in us and empowers us to live for Him. Our job, then, is to depend daily upon His strength as we seek to achieve victory over the sin and darkness that tempt us to disobey Christ.

Walking in dependence upon God's Spirit demands our active participation in the spiritual disciplines. These disciplines do not, in and of themselves, make us holy. But they do make us available and open to the Spirit's transforming power. For each of the disciplines that follow, describe what you currently do on a daily, weekly, or monthly basis.

- Study the Word

- Memorize Scripture

- Pray

- Worship God privately and with other believers

- Give to God's kingdom financially or through your service

- Fast from food or from some other acceptable thing

10. Look at the list again. What disciplines do you need to grow in? What specifically will you do differently this coming week? Who will hold you accountable?

11. Often when God provides us with victory, we forget to thank Him. We'll see in the next lesson how dangerous ingratitude toward God can be. In the space that follows, write a prayer of thanks to God for His Spirit and for any spiritual victories He has already allowed you to achieve.

MEMORIZE

For this week, memorize Romans 8:11:

> **And if the Spirit of him who raised Jesus from the dead is living in you, he who raised Christ from the dead will also give life to your mortal bodies through his Spirit, who lives in you. (NIV)**

Leaving a Legacy

From everlasting to everlasting the LORD's love is with those who fear him, and his righteousness with their children's children.

PSALM 103:17 (NIV)

WE OWE A great debt to Jonathan Edwards, arguably the greatest American theologian in history. His sermons and books ignited the First Great Awakening, an American revival in the mid-1700s that brought thousands of men and women to faith and moved many others to a deeper walk with the Lord. Even today, countless Christians continue to gain insight and inspiration through his writings.

What many people don't know about Edwards, however, is that he left behind an amazing family legacy. In 1900, a researcher studied nearly 1,400 descendants of Jonathan and Sarah Edwards. He found that among them were more than 100 lawyers, 30 judges, 13 college presidents, 60 doctors, one United States vice president, 80 public officials, 60 authors, and 100 in vocational ministry as pastors, missionaries, or theological professors![1] Few families could claim such an impressive legacy.

How did one man have that kind of effect on his descendants for so many generations? He and his wife, Sarah, were certainly intelligent and hardworking. But more important, they passionately followed the Lord and intentionally trained their eleven children to do the same. Despite a heavy load of ministry responsibilities, Edwards took an active role in the training and discipline of his kids, and he faithfully taught them to know the Bible and to serve the Lord. As a result, many of his descendants became men and women who loved Jesus and invested their lives in serving Him.

Unfortunately, not everyone leaves such a wonderful legacy. The Bible is filled with stories of men, like Gideon, who began the race well but limped across the finish line. Sadly, Gideon's life demonstrates the tragic consequences of finishing poorly, of failing to leave a godly legacy. Read Judges 8:22-35:

> The Israelites said, "Rule over us, you and your son and your grandson. You have saved us from Midian's tyranny."
>
> Gideon said, "I most certainly will not rule over you, nor will my son. GOD will reign over you."
>
> Then Gideon said, "But I do have one request. Give me, each of you, an earring that you took as plunder." Ishmaelites wore gold earrings, and the men all had their pockets full of them.
>
> They said, "Of course. They're yours!"
>
> They spread out a blanket and each man threw his plundered earrings on it. The gold earrings that Gideon had asked for weighed about forty-three pounds—and that didn't include the crescents and pendants, the purple robes worn by the Midianite kings, and the ornaments hung around the necks of their camels.
>
> Gideon made the gold into a sacred ephod and put it on display in his hometown, Ophrah. All Israel prostituted itself there. Gideon and his family, too, were seduced by it.
>
> Midian's tyranny was broken by the Israelites; nothing more was heard from them. The land was quiet for forty years in Gideon's time.

Jerub-Baal son of Joash went home and lived in his house. Gideon had seventy sons. He fathered them all—he had a lot of wives! His concubine, the one at Shechem, also bore him a son. He named him Abimelech.

Gideon son of Joash died at a good old age. He was buried in the tomb of his father Joash at Ophrah of the Abiezrites.

Gideon was hardly cool in the tomb when the People of Israel had gotten off track and were prostituting themselves to Baal—they made Baal-of-the-Covenant their god. The People of Israel forgot all about GOD, their God, who had saved them from all their enemies who had hemmed them in. And they didn't keep faith with the family of Jerub-Baal (Gideon), honoring all the good he had done for Israel.

CONSIDERING YOUR OWN LEGACY

1. Our legacy is not only the impact we will have on our children one day but also the effect of our lives on everybody in our sphere of influence. Make a list of the people who are affected by the choices you make, now and in the future.

2. Evaluate your choices (now and in the past) in the chart that follows. Which ones are likely to lead to a positive legacy, and which are likely to lead to a negative legacy?

Positive Choices	Negative Choices

LOOK IT OVER

Gideon and the Israelites experienced an amazing victory through God's power. However, the great victory seems to have changed Gideon for the worse. When we first met him, he was insecure and frightened but willing to take a great step of faith in order to obey God. After the victory, though, he became arrogant and hungry for power. As we look carefully at the passage for this week, we can identify three sinful decisions that Gideon made that ended up destroying his legacy. First, he asked the Israelite soldiers for their gold as a tribute to him as their leader. Second, he set up an ephod that ended up becoming an idol to the nation (more on that later). Finally, he named his son Abimelech, which means "my father is king," an indication of Gideon's true feelings about himself. All three decisions were subtle but powerful ways in which

Gideon communicated that his priorities were not consistent with God's desire for his life.

»»

AMASSING A FORTUNE

The Israelites gave Gideon 1,700 shekels of gold, in addition to a number of other treasures. The gold alone weighed around 43 pounds. At the time we are writing this study, the value in today's dollars of that much gold is around $962,000!

3. What is the significance of Gideon receiving tribute after the battle by asking his men for their gold (see Deuteronomy 17:14-17; 1 Samuel 8:10-18)? What was he communicating by this request?

4. What was the effect of the ephod on Gideon, his family, and his country?

Because the ephod was a means of communication with God, over time it became a symbol for God Himself, and some Israelites even began to worship it as a god. Gideon's golden ephod is an example of this; he fashioned an idol, an image created to represent God, and the people sinned by worshipping it. By making the ephod, Gideon was claiming for himself a high privilege: that of acting as the high priest, or mediator, between God and the people. Unfortunately, God had not appointed him to that role, and by claiming it he brought terrible consequences to his family and his nation.

5. Gideon named his son Abimelech, which means "my father is king" (see Judges 8:31). Why is this significant in light of Gideon's response when the people asked him to be king (see 8:22-23)?

THINK IT THROUGH

6. What do Gideon's actions after the battle tell you about his attitude toward God?

7. Through his actions after the battle, Gideon amassed a substantial fortune. Is it sinful to accumulate wealth? What are the dangers inherent in wealth (see Proverbs 30:8-9; 1 Timothy 6:6-10)?

8. Gideon arrogantly claimed the authority of a high priest when he created the ephod. Many generations later, a king of Judah named Uzziah, who had been faithful to the Lord for most of his life, made the same prideful claim. Read 2 Chronicles 26:16-21. What were the consequences of Uzziah's claim to priestly authority? Why did God take this sin so seriously?

9. Read the following selections from Judges 9, which discuss the short and tragic career of Gideon's son Abimelech. Underline all of the negative consequences of Abimelech's kingly ambitions.

Abimelech son of Jerub-Baal went to Shechem to his uncles and all his mother's relatives and said to them, "Ask all the leading men of Shechem, 'What do you think is best, that seventy men rule you—all those sons of Jerub-Baal—or that one man rule? You'll remember that I am your own flesh and blood.'"

His mother's relatives reported the proposal to the leaders of Shechem. They were inclined to take Abimelech. "Because," they said, "he is, after all, one of us."

They gave him seventy silver pieces from the shrine of Baal-of-the-Covenant. With the money he hired some reckless riffraff soldiers and they followed along after him. He went to his father's house in Ophrah and killed his half brothers, the sons of Jerub-Baal—seventy men! And on one stone! The youngest, Jotham son of Jerub-Baal, managed to hide, the only survivor.

Then all the leaders of Shechem and Beth Millo gathered at the Oak by the Standing Stone at Shechem and crowned Abimelech king. . . .

Abimelech ruled over Israel for three years. Then God brought bad blood between Abimelech and Shechem's leaders, who now worked treacherously behind his back. Violence boomeranged: The murderous violence that killed the seventy brothers, the sons of Jerub-Baal, was now loose among Abimelech and Shechem's leaders, who had supported the violence. . . .

Gaal son of Ebed said, "Who is this Abimelech? And who are we Shechemites to take orders from him? Isn't he the son of Jerub-Baal, and isn't this his henchman Zebul? We belong to the race of Hamor and bear the noble name of Shechem. Why should we be toadies of Abimelech? If I were in charge of this people, the first thing I'd do is get rid of Abimelech! I'd say, 'Show me your stuff, Abimelech—let's see who's boss here!'". . .

The next day the people went out to the fields. This was reported to Abimelech. He took his troops, divided them into three companies, and placed them in ambush in the fields. When he saw that the people were well out in the open, he sprang up and attacked them. Abimelech and the company with him charged ahead and took control of the entrance to the city gate; the other two companies chased down those who were in the open fields and killed them. Abimelech fought at the city all that day. He captured the city and massacred everyone in it. He leveled the city to the ground, then sowed it with salt. . . .

Abimelech went on to Thebez. He camped at Thebez and captured it. The Tower-of-Strength stood in the middle of the city; all the men and women of the city along with the city's leaders had fled there and locked themselves in. They were up on the tower roof. Abimelech got as far as the tower and assaulted it. He came up to the tower door to set it on fire. Just then some woman dropped an upper millstone on his head and crushed his skull. He called urgently to his young armor bearer and said, "Draw your sword and kill me so they can't say of me, 'A woman killed him.'" His armor bearer drove in his sword, and Abimelech died.

When the Israelites saw that Abimelech was dead, they went home.

God avenged the evil Abimelech had done to his father, murdering his seventy brothers. (verses 1-6,22-24,28-29,42-45, 50-56)

10. According to Judges 8 and 9, what were the negative consequences of Gideon's actions for his family and for the nation? List them in the space that follows.

MAKE IT REAL

11. Think about a good decision you made in the recent past. What were the effects of that decision for your family, friends, and others in your life?

12. Think about a poor decision you made in the recent past. What were the effects of that decision for your family, friends, and others in your life?

All of us will leave behind a legacy when we die. It might be a legacy of godliness and love, or it might be a legacy of unrighteousness and pain. As we close our study of Gideon, spend some time thinking about the legacy you would like to leave behind. In the space that follows, write your own eulogy. What do you hope people will say about you at your funeral? How do you want to be remembered?

My Eulogy

13. What changes do you need to make in your life to become someone who leaves behind the kind of legacy you hope to leave?

MEMORIZE

For this week, memorize Proverbs 20:7:

The righteous who walks in his integrity — blessed are his children after him! (ESV)

Throughout this study, we've been able to learn more about trusting God at all times, even in difficult situations, instead of relying on our own strengths and abilities. He desires to give our lives significance and makes it possible for us to do extraordinary things through the power of His Spirit. Take the next few minutes to pray about all that you learned from Gideon's story about God's faithfulness and His desires for us. Ask Him to continue helping you overcome anything that may be holding you back from trusting Him.

Leader's Guide

WE'RE GLAD THAT you have decided to lead your group through this study of the life of Gideon. We pray that God will use this study to transform you and the students in your group into more faithful servants of Him. The Word of God is powerful when it is studied in the context of a Christian community who can challenge us to obedience.

The degree to which a small group understands and applies the Scripture is ultimately dependent on the work of the Holy Spirit. However, the leader has a critical role in helping the group listen carefully to God's Word. Your role, then, is to constantly point your group back to the Scripture and to challenge them to understand and apply it.

LESSON FORMAT

Each lesson of this study is broken down into four major sections (this format is loosely based on the inductive Bible study methodology outlined in *Living by the Book*, by Howard and William Hendricks[1]):

Introduction/Need: Every lesson begins with an opening story designed to stir interest in the subject and to relate the main point of the passage to a real-life situation. Following the written introduction, we have included a few questions just to provoke some initial thought about the week's topic. Our goal in this section is simply to help the student see the need to study the passage and to introduce perhaps one or two ways in which the passage might be personally relevant.

Look It Over: This section is designed to stimulate observation directly from the text. The purpose of these questions is not to inquire about the *meaning* of the text (the next section will accomplish that goal), but instead just to observe what the passage actually *says*. As a leader, you'll want to continually challenge the group to ground their observations in the biblical text. One temptation at this stage will be for you or other group members to jump ahead to application. For example, if the passage talks about the idolatry of the Israelites and how they incurred God's judgment, it might be tempting here to say, "We worship idols also. What are our idols and how can we avoid them?" That's an application question; save those sorts of inquiries for the final section, "Make It Real." Instead, at this stage focus on questions related to the text itself: "What did the people do that made God so angry?" or "What was God's response to the Israelites' practice of idolatry?" By studying the passage carefully, your group will be better prepared to understand and apply it.

Think It Through: This portion of the study is designed to take students deeper into the text through the process of interpretation. Sometimes there are difficult questions that we need to answer before we can apply the text. For instance, the world of the Bible was quite different from our own. As a result, you might need to walk your group through a bit of background study or look up a few cross-references. Where necessary, we've provided dialogue boxes with critical information to help you in this process. For example, it helps to understand the nature of idolatry in the ancient world so we can understand what idolatry looks like today and how we can avoid it. Continue to resist the temptation to apply the text at this point; instead, help your group understand what it means (not what it means *to you or to the students* but what it actually means *in light of the original context*).

Make It Real: The final section of each lesson is designed to encourage personal application of the text. Every passage of Scripture, even those that seem the strangest to us today, contains principles that are timeless and can be applied to our lives. To that end, we've provided questions and exercises to prompt the students to reflect on their own lives, identify where they are falling short, and make a specific plan for growth. Don't let your group members leave their applications general

("I will be more thankful to God"); help them make specific, concrete plans ("I will grow in thankfulness by spending at least five minutes each day this week writing down specific things I am thankful to God for"). As the leader, consider organizing group activities for some of the applications. Students (especially young men) often connect with one another and learn best in an active setting, so you might plan service projects, road trips, or other events to help with the application process. We also encourage group accountability. Don't allow the applications to be forgotten after the discussion for each lesson, but instead return to them in subsequent weeks to help your group hold one another accountable.

At the end of each lesson, we have included a memory verse. We encourage you to have your group members recite these each week. However, if memorizing all of the verses is too overwhelming, pick one or two and focus on them throughout the course of the study. For example, Psalm 20:7, used at the end of lesson 1, is a good summary verse for the entire study of Gideon's life. Each group member can memorize that verse and simply repeat it each week to help solidify the main point of this study, namely that a godly person trusts in the Lord rather than in his own strength or ability.

STRUCTURING YOUR TIME

Depending on the topic, the composition of your group, and their level of preparation, your group time might be structured in several different ways. We recommend that you allow at least an hour for your group meetings, and more time if possible. Assuming that your group has about an hour to meet, here is a suggested timeline (adjust this proportionately if you have more or less time each week):

- *5–10 minutes:* Welcome and prayer
- *5–10 minutes:* Introduction/Need
- *10–15 minutes:* Look It Over
- *15–20 minutes:* Think It Through
- *10–15 minutes:* Make It Real

We recognize that it is often challenging to answer all of the questions in your allotted time. If one question or concept generates a great deal of discussion, it's not always wise to end the dialogue simply to move on to the next question. As the leader, use your discretion to determine whether to allow a "rabbit trail" or to gently encourage the group to move on to a different topic. Consider carefully whether a particular discussion is the most productive use of time for the entire group. If an issue is troubling one member more than the others, offer to meet with him or her individually at a different time. That will allow you to continue with the study in a way that meets the needs of all members.

Nothing energizes a Bible study like challenging questions. Though we've included many questions in the book, we encourage you to go beyond them. Brainstorm questions of your own from the passage to ask your group. Include "devil's advocate" questions, where you take a counter-position and force your group to defend their views from Scripture. Many students, especially guys, love debate, so don't hesitate to dial up the tension in your meetings!

If your group has not prepared ahead of time, begin by reading the lesson's passage with them and encouraging them to verbally make observations. You might want to provide some initial observations and thoughts on the passage for your group just to get them started. You can write their observations on a dry-erase board, project them onto a screen, or have the group members write them in their own books. After spending a few minutes observing, challenge them to answer the most critical questions from "Think It Through" on the spot. Finally, prompt them to think through how they might apply the text this coming week.

Most important, do not skip the "Make It Real" portion of the study in the interest of time. Ultimately, the effectiveness of a Bible study is measured by the impact it has on the group members' lives, not by the knowledge it generates. If you are short on time, move quickly through the "Look It Over" and "Think It Through" sections so you have time to discuss application.

THEMES AND KEY QUESTIONS FOR EACH LESSON

As we mentioned earlier, the primary goal of this study is to encourage group members to trust God, rather than their own strengths or abilities, in the challenging times of life. Gideon had to learn that God's power infinitely surpassed his own and more than compensated for even his greatest weaknesses. He was tested in this area of trust both in good times and in tough times; sometimes he responded well, but other times he failed. Each week, bring your group back to this issue of trusting in God as the key point of the entire study. We must learn to trust Him not only for our salvation but also in every area of our daily lives.

Each lesson of the study will contribute to that idea in a different way. Here are the themes and critical questions to answer for each lesson of the study:

Lesson 1: Spend some time talking about what it means to be a hero. Is a true hero a macho man who can do it all, or is a true hero someone who trusts in the Lord for victory? The real need in our culture, as in Gideon's day, is for people who will trust God as they seek to make a difference in the world. You might have some students in your group who do not yet have a relationship with Christ; emphasize that the beginning of a life of true impact is trusting in Jesus for forgiveness of their sins and eternal life. For those who already believe, help them understand that faith does not end at the gospel. Every day, we succeed or fail as followers of Christ based on our faith in God's power and promises.

If you find yourself running short on time, skim through the "Think It Through" questions related to idolatry and focus primarily on how a true hero in God's economy is the person who trusts Him.

Lesson 2: The critical point to emphasize in this lesson is that sin begins with a value system that is opposed to the values of God. Overcoming sin requires exercising faith in God's power and in His value system. Many, if not most, of those in your group will be struggling with repetitive sin issues such as pornography, pride, and anger. Create a safe environment in which they can discuss those challenges, and encourage them to evaluate the reasons for their struggles. Challenge them to take the necessary steps to move away from sin and toward a closer walk with Christ. Some of them might need to limit their Internet access or reconsider which friends they spend time with. Help them set up accountability with you or with one another. Ideally you will continue to encourage them and hold them accountable even after the eight-week study has ended. If you are short on time, spend less time on questions 8–10.

Lesson 3: This lesson focuses on the fears we face as followers of Christ and the courage we can gain from the promises of God. Gideon was called to a task for which he was personally inadequate, and he was afraid. Encourage group members to explore their own fears about obeying God. Do they fear ridicule, failure, loneliness, or something else? How can we overcome those fears and trust in God? If you are short on time this week, you can skip questions 4 and 9.

Lesson 4: Spend most of your time this week thinking about the nature of idolatry in our culture. The key to understanding is to help your group see that an idol is anything we value more than we value God. Consequently, we often worship idols with our bodies, hearts, and minds even though we don't overtly bow down to them. What are the idols that tempt your group members, and what steps must they take to make God the center of their worship? If you are short on time, focus on the "Think It Through" and "Make It Real" portions of the study and spend a bit less time on "Look It Over."

Lesson 5: This lesson discusses the clear instructions God had given to Gideon and how he was still afraid to fully trust the Lord. Emphasize the nature of God's character (absolutely trustworthy) and talk about some of the promises He has made to us in the Bible. God has promised Christians the power to overcome sin, the ability to share the gospel effectively, and a number of other blessings. How can your group step out in faith, responding to the clear call of God on their lives? If you are short on time, skim through questions 6–8 and focus more time on the "Make It Real" portion of the lesson.

Lesson 6: In this lesson's passage, we see how God eliminated any chance for Gideon or the Israelites to trust in the size or skill of their army. God forced Gideon and Israel to trust only in Him for victory. Sometimes God's plans seem risky, or even crazy, but He can always be trusted. Our temptation, though, is to rely on ourselves instead of on God, believing that our plan is better. Spend a good portion of your time focusing on exactly how God worked with Gideon and how it relates to us. God's plan for Gideon is a good example of how God demands that we trust Him and give Him all of the glory for every victory. If you are short on time, skim through questions 6, 8, and 11. You can also spend a bit less time on the "Make It Real" section this week since it will connect closely to the applications in lesson 7.

Lesson 7: There are fewer questions in this lesson than in most of the others, so your group will likely have time to discuss them all. The key idea of the passage is how God used a very strange battle plan to provide victory. The victory was won completely through God's power and not through the might of Gideon's army. As Christians, the Holy Spirit lives within us to provide us spiritual victory. We experience victory over sin and the Devil as we rely on the Spirit. The "Make It Real" section emphasizes Romans 8:11, which talks of the power of God's Spirit. Challenge your students to consider how they can rely on the Spirit's power through prayer, studying the Scripture, and connecting with a community of other Christians. Encourage them to pray specifically for the Lord to provide victory in an area of their spiritual life, and then have them share during your final week of the study how God has responded to their prayers.

Lesson 8: This final lesson emphasizes the concept of leaving a godly legacy. Gideon became arrogant after his victory over the Midianites. Sadly, he left behind a legacy of idolatry and violence rather than peace and trust in God. The most important part of this lesson for your group is included in the "Make It Real" section. Make sure your group members spend time writing their own eulogies and considering how they can leave behind a legacy of faithfulness to God. Share your eulogies as a group and encourage one another to begin building lives that reflect those eulogies. If you are short on time, this is the one part of the study that you don't want to skip!

"GOD IS WITH YOU, O MIGHTY WARRIOR!"

We pray that God will use you, just as He used Gideon, to accomplish great things for His glory and the good of His people. We pray that your group will grow closer to the Lord through this study and that each person will learn how to trust Him in deeper ways. We're confident that His Spirit will be at work in your group as you consistently direct them to His Word. For further resources, feel free to look at Grace Bible Church's website, www.grace-bible.org, or contact NavPress at www.navpress.com. And don't forget to check out the other studies in the ORDINARY GREATNESS series.

Notes

LESSON 4: SMASHING THE IDOLS

1. Paul J. Achtemeier, ed., *Harper's Bible Dictionary* (San Francisco: Harper & Row, 1985), 84.
2. Anthony Umrani, "Sacred Spaces: Inside a Hindu Temple," *CNN Belief Blog,* June 25, 2011, http://religion.blogs.cnn.com/2011/06/25/sacred-space-inside-a-hindu-temple/.

LESSON 5: CONFIDENCE IN GOD'S CALLING

1. Anthony B. Wong, "Report on 'The Cambridge Seven,'" *Wholesome Words,* 2011, http://www.wholesomewords.org/missions/bcambridge7.html.

LESSON 6: RELYING ON GOD'S STRENGTH

1. "History," The Alamo, accessed October 19, 2011, http://www.thealamo.org/battle/battle.php.
2. Mike Cox, "Line in the Sand," TexasEscapes.com accessed December 6, 2011, http://www.texasescapes.com/MikeCoxTexasTales/Line-in-the-Sand-Alamo-History.htm.
3. "History," The Alamo, http://www.thealamo.org/battle/battle.php.
4. Stephen L. Hardin, "Battle of the Alamo," *The Handbook of Texas Online,* Texas State Historical Association, accessed November 15, 2011, http://www.tshaonline.org/handbook/online/articles/qea02.

LESSON 7: HOW UNDERDOGS BECOME VICTORIOUS

1. "Miracle on Ice," *Wikipedia,* accessed August 29, 2011, http://en.wikipedia.org/wiki/Miracle_on_Ice.

LESSON 8: LEAVING A LEGACY

1. George Marsden, *Jonathan Edwards: A Life* (New Haven, CT: Yale University Press, 2003), 500–501.

LEADER'S GUIDE

1. Howard and William Hendricks, *Living by the Book* (Chicago: Moody, 1991).

About the Authors

Matt Morton, Brian Fisher, and Blake Jennings serve together at Grace Bible Church in College Station, Texas. GBC is a multisite church of four thousand people located near Texas A&M University. Because of the church's focus on the next generation of spiritual leaders, more than two thousand students attend weekly college worship times and participate in weekly Bible studies, discipleship, and summer missions opportunities.

Matt is the college pastor of GBC's Anderson Campus. He graduated from Dallas Theological Seminary and Texas A&M University. He and his wife, Shannon, have three wonderful children.

Brian serves as the senior pastor of GBC. He holds a master's degree and a doctorate from Dallas Theological Seminary and is a graduate of Texas A&M University. He is married to Tristie. They have two beautiful children.

Blake is the teaching pastor of GBC's Southwood Campus. He graduated from Dallas Theological Seminary and Texas A&M University. He and his wife, Julie, are the proud parents of Gracie and Luke.

MY LIFE IS **TOUGHER** THAN MOST **PEOPLE REALIZE.**

I TRY TO
KEEP EVERYTHING
IN BALANCE:
FRIENDS, FAMILY, WORK,
SCHOOL, AND GOD.

IT'S NOT EASY.

I KNOW WHAT MY
PARENTS BELIEVE AND
WHAT MY PASTOR SAYS.

BUT IT'S NOT
ABOUT THEM.
IT'S ABOUT ME...

ISN'T IT TIME I
OWN MY FAITH?

THROUGH THICK AND THIN, KEEP YOUR HEARTS AT ATTENTION, IN
ADORATION BEFORE CHRIST, YOUR MASTER. BE READY TO SPEAK
UP AND TELL ANYONE WHO ASKS WHY YOU'RE LIVING THE WAY
YOU ARE, AND ALWAYS WITH THE UTMOST COURTESY. I PETER 3:15 (MSG)

www.navpress.com | 1-800-366-7788

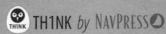

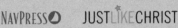

The Message Means Understanding

Bringing the Bible to all ages

he Message is written in contemporary language that is much like talking with a good friend. When paired with your favorite Bible study, *The Message* will deliver a reading experience that is reliable, energetic, and amazingly fresh.